D1598119

REALISM
AND
NOMINALISM
REVISITED

The Aquinas Lecture, 1954

REALISM
AND
NOMINALISM
REVISITED

Under the Auspices of the Aristotelian Society
of Marquette University

BY

HENRY VEATCH, Ph.D.

MARQUETTE UNIVERSITY PRESS
MILWAUKEE
1954

Prefatory

The Aristotelian Society of Marquette University each year invites a scholar to deliver a lecture in honor of St. Thomas Aquinas. Customarily delivered on the Sunday nearest March 7, the feast day of the Society's patron saint, these lectures are called the Aquinas lectures.

In 1954 the Society had the pleasure of recording the lecture of Henry Babcock Veatch, Ph.D., professor of philosophy at Indiana University.

Born in Evansville, Indiana, in 1911, he received his primary education in the public schools of that city. He then attended Phillips Exeter Academy and Harvard University, receiving his A.B. degree with honors in 1932 and a master's degree in philosophy in 1933. He spent two years in study at the University of Heidelberg on a Phillip Sears traveling fellowship from Harvard. Returning from abroad, Dr. Veatch resumed study at Harvard and received his Ph.D. degree in 1936. After a year as an assistant in philosophy at Harvard he joined the philosophy faculty of Indiana University. There he served successively as instructor (1937-41), assistant professor (1941-48), associate professor (1948-52), and since 1952 as full professor. Dr. Veatch was awarded a fellowship in 1952 by the Ford Foundation Fund for Advancement of Education and spent a year in the study of the relation between philosophy and religion at the Pontifical Institute of Mediaeval Studies, Toronto, and the Harvard Divinity School.

Dr. Veatch is a member of the American Philosophical Association, Association for Realistic Philosophy, Mind Association, Indiana Philosophical Association, and Phi Beta Kappa.

In 1952 Yale University Press published his work, *Intentional Logic*. He has contributed the chapter on Aristotelianism for *A History of Philosophical*

Systems, (Vergilius Ture Anselm Ferm, editor, Philosophical Library, New York, 1950) and the chapter on logic for another philosophical volume, *Return To Reason,* (John Wild, editor, Henry Regnery, Chicago, 1953). He also has written a number of articles and reviews for philosophy journals.

To the list of his writings the Aristotelian Society has the honor of adding *Realism and Nominalism Revisited.*

Acknowledgements

Much of the material of this lecture was presented originally in a short paper read before the Association for Realistic Philosophy, in the spring of 1953 at Brown University, and later in two lectures delivered under the auspices of the Faculté de Philosophie, Université Laval, Québec, during the summer of 1953. On both occasions I profited greatly from the discussions that followed, and I should like to express my thanks to participants and sponsors alike.

But even more particularly, my gratitude goes out to the Reverend Gerard Smith, S.J., and his colleagues at Marquette University for any number of pertinent comments and suggestions, to say nothing of their most gracious hospitality during my stay in Milwaukee.

> "I can no other answer make but thanks,
> And thanks; and ever . . . oft good turns
> Are shuffled off with such uncurrent pay:
> But, were my worth as is my conscience firm,
> You should find better dealing."

Realism and Nominalism Revisited

REALISM and nominalism may well be perennial issues in philosophy. And yet in a celebrated lecture, entitled "Logicism and Philosophy,"[1] delivered in Harvard University some 18 years ago, Professor Gilson would seem to have implied that at certain times and in certain situations in the history of philosophy the issue between realists and nominalists is likely to be much more acute than at others. Specifically, Professor Gilson was talking about the 12th century, and he was contending that the almost hopeless philosophical impasse that was the result of the realist-nominalist controversy of those days might in large measure have been due to the fact that the thinkers of the 12th century knew little else in philosophy save logic, and they accordingly undertook to solve all philosophical problems, even those of metaphysics, not as metaphysicians, but simply as logicians.[2]

Now without pressing the parallel too far, it may none-the-less be significant for us to note that today, no less than in the 12th century, there is a realist-nominalist controversy raging.[3] Not only that, but most of the parties to the present dispute are men who would no doubt call themselves, if not logicians, at least semanticists; and in any case they would all be pretty much agreed that the only really serious discipline in philosophy is logic.[4] Accordingly, one cannot but wonder whether, just as it was logicism that was at the root of the realist-nominalist controversy in the 12th century, it may not also be a kind of logicism that is at the root of the contemporary dispute in semantics between the so-called

Platonists[5] on the one hand, and the self-styled nominalists on the other.

At any rate, in this present lecture the thesis that I should like to advance—in all tentativeness and diffidence, to be sure —is that the current issue of realism vs. nominalism may be in large measure understood in terms of, and perhaps may even be said to have been caused by, the rather uncritical use by modern logicians of a certain basic schema,[6] or ordering pattern, that quite literally dominates the entire vast corpus of modern mathematical logic. The schema or basic pattern to which I refer is that of function and argument, and the person who first made extensive use of such a schema in the field of logic was the great 19th century German mathematician, Gottlob Frege. Of course, the notions themselves of function and argument had long been current in mathematics before Frege, but their usage there, Frege thought, had been regrettably loose and misleading. Accordingly, he set about to give the notions a precise and definite meaning. Here is his own account of the matter:

> People . . . recognize the same function again in
>
> $$\text{'}2.1^3+1,\text{'}$$
> $$\text{'}2.4^3+4,\text{'}$$
> $$\text{'}2.5^3+5,\text{'}$$
>
> only with different arguments, viz. 1, 4, and 5. From this we may discern that it is the common element of these expressions that contains the essential peculiarity of a function; i.e., what is present in
>
> $$\text{'}2.x^3+x\text{'}$$
>
> over and above the letter 'x.' We could write this somewhat as follows:
>
> $$\text{'}2.(\ )^3+(\ )\text{'}.^7$$

So much for function. As for the notion of argument, Frege continues in the same passage as follows:

> I am concerned to show that the argument does not belong with the function, but goes together with the function to make up a complete whole; for the function by itself must be called incomplete, in need of supplementation, or 'unsatu-

rated.' And in this respect functions differ fundamentally from numbers . . . We now see how people are easily led to regard the form of the expression as what is essential to the function. We recognize the function in the expression by imagining the latter as split up, and the possibility of thus splitting it up is suggested by its structure.

The two parts into which the mathematical expression is thus split up, the sign of the argument and the expression of the function, are dissimilar; for the argument is a number, a whole complete in itself, as the function is not.[8]

Nevertheless, Frege's purpose was not restricted to offering merely a more rigorous and accurate account of the mathematical notions of function and argument. In addition, he proposed to generalize these notions so as to make them applicable far beyond the confines of mathematics in the narrower sense. Specifically, he proposed to use them in the analysis of concepts and propositions in logic. Thus he says:

Statements in general, just like equations or inequalities or expressions in Analysis, can be imagined to be split up into two parts; one complete in itself, and the other in need of supplementation, or 'unsaturated.' Thus, e.g., we split up the sentence.

'Caesar conquered Gaul'

into 'Caesar' and 'conquered Gaul.' The second part is 'unsaturated'—it contains an empty place; only when this place is filled up with a proper name, does a complete sense appear. Here too I give the name 'function' to what this 'unsaturated' part stands for. In this case the argument is Caesar.[9]

Now at first glance all this may seem plausible enough. Why not use the schema of function and argument as a device for analyzing concepts and propositions? It seems harmless enough and, one might be tempted to add, rather insignificant too.

However, whatever may be one's ultimate decision on the innocence or harmfulness of this rather simple schema, it must certainly not be adjudged insignificant. For no sooner was it introduced into logic than it seems to have swept all before it. For one thing, not only did predication of the traditional type appear to lend itself to analysis in terms of this schema, but also relations as well. Thus a predicate such as 'red' can very readily be regarded as an unsaturated function, 'x is red,' which will become saturated as soon as an argument is given to replace the variable 'x.' But so also a relation such as 'greater than' can be set up as an unsaturated function, 'x is greater than y.' This time, though, the function will require two arguments for its saturation or fulfillment. Hence it may be appropriately called a two-place function.

On the same principle, too, 'x gave y to z' would be a three-place function. And from three-place functions we may go on to imagine four-place, five-place, and so on up to n-place functions.

But having got this far, we already

find that the stage is set for the vast and elaborate quantification theory of modern logic, a theory, which it is claimed, almost infinitely surpasses the old subject-predicate theory of traditional logic in range and power. Thus each one of these so-called one-place, two-place, and so on up to n-place functions may be regarded as being quite literally a *propositional* function. That is to say, each is an unfulfilled or unsaturated function, which upon fulfillment becomes a proposition. And fulfillment may come about either by giving specific values to the variables of the function, or else by "binding" or "quantifying" the variables, as it is called.[10]

Nor would there seem to be much doubt that such a theory of the proposition is certainly much more all-embracing than the traditional subject-predicate theory. Indeed, what is a subject-predicate proposition but the fulfillment or saturation of a simple one-place function, whereas the propositions envisaged in quantification theory will involve besides one-place functions, two-place, three-place, four-place and so on up to n-place functions!

Nor do the seven-league boots of this extraordinary function-argument schema come to rest here. On the contrary, one more step, and the entire traditional doctrine of compound or hypothetical propositions is not only covered, but covered in such a way that the whole area is seen to have a hitherto unsuspected complexity, and at the same time to be susceptible of an orderly arranging and mapping that had never even been thought of before, much less carried out. Thus take typical propositional conjunctions such as 'if-then,' 'or,' 'and,' etc. Why may not these be regarded as just so many unsaturated or unfulfilled functions, the arguments this time being nothing more nor less than whole propositions? Once more, it is an enticing project that is presented. Nor have the results of the

project lagged behind its initial promise.
For these results are comprised in that
detailed and elaborate achievement of
modern logic that has come to be known
as the propositional or truth-functional
calculus.

Apparently, then, there would seem
to be no disputing the fact: Frege's proposal to introduce the mathematical
notions of function and argument into
logic, so far from being of minor significance, has actually had the effect of com-
pletely revolutionizing logic. For example,
Bertrand Russell, not long after the turn
of the century, became so intoxicated with
the potentialities of this new schema or
device for the analysis of logical entities
like propositions that he was not merely
willing to brush aside the whole of traditional logic: "since it holds that all
propositions have the subject-predicate
form, (it) is unable to admit the reality of
relations."[11] In addition, he was moved
to give to the very essay in which these

strictures against the older logic appeared the resounding title of "Logic as the Essence of Philosophy." And elsewhere and in the same vein, he indulged in the most sweeping claims for the new logic. "The true function of logic as applied to matters of experience," he says, is to "show the possibility of hitherto unsuspected alternatives," to "liberate the imagination as to what the world *may* be."[12] For "logic is concerned with the analysis and enumeration of logical *forms*, i.e., . . . with the various types of facts, and with the classification of the constituents of facts. In this way logic provides an inventory of possibilities, a repertory of abstractly tenable hypotheses."[13]

And now let us look away briefly from this rather dazzling spectacle of a logic erected on the basis of the function-argument schema and conceived on a truly grand scale, to consider a much more modest and somewhat forgotten view of logic. In his Commentary on Aristotle's

Metaphysics, St. Thomas Aquinas has occasion to refer to the distinction between *ens rationis* and *ens naturae;* and in this connection he makes a very illuminating suggestion as to the proper subject matter of logic:

> The notion of a being of reason is properly attributed to those intentions which reason finds in things insofar as they are considered by reason—such for instance as the intention of genus, of species, and the like which, to be sure, are not found *in rerum natura,* but rather are consequent upon reason's consideration of the things of nature. Now it is this sort of thing (scil. *ens rationis*) that is properly the subject of logic.[14]

This is a very brief passage, to be sure, and yet it does not leave much room for doubt or equivocation: if the subject matter of logic is the sort of thing which St. Thomas here suggests that it is, then it is quite obviously not the sort of thing that Lord Russell says it is. Liberating the imagination, or drawing up inventories of possibilities, or contemplating unsuspected alternatives as to what in the eyes of God or chance or the devil or Lord Russell the world may be—all this is all very well, but it simply isn't the business of logic, at least not according to St. Thomas. For the possibilities that Lord Russell would have logic disclose and reveal are real possibilities; they are not mere intentions in the sense of beings of reason.

Moreover, unless I be much mistaken, the reason the function-argument schema of modern logic has given rise so readily to a realist-nominalist controversy is precisely because such a schema does not partake of the character of a logical intention in St. Thomas' sense at all. Accordingly, before we can very well expose the peculiar weakness of this type of schema, we must first get clear as to just what this feature of intentionality is which, St. Thomas seems to feel, all properly logical entities must have,[15] but which, as we are going to suggest, is just what the function-argument schema lacks.

Now to judge by the brief quotation from St. Thomas, the first criterion of intentionality in a logical sense is that, so far from pertaining to anything in the natural world, whether actual or merely possible, intentionality is wholly consequent upon reason's consideration of the things of nature. That is to say, it is only insofar as things come to be known, or better, it is only insofar as in coming to be known they acquire a status as objects of thought or reason, that they therewith take on certain characteristics or "intentions" which otherwise and just in themselves they would not have at all. For instance, we might suppose it simply a fact that hydrogen has an atomic weight of 1.008. Nevertheless, insofar as we come to know this fact in regard to hydrogen, we make 'hydrogen' the subject of a proposition and we predicate 'having an atomic weight of 1.008' of it. Accordingly, being the subject of a proposition is an example of an "intention" which, to paraphrase St. Thomas, reason may be said to find[16] in hydrogen, insofar as hydrogen comes to be known and is made an object before the mind.

Nevertheless, there is a second criterion of logical intentionality which, while it is intimately connected with the first, is perhaps even more important than the first. True, this second criterion is not one that is explicitly mentioned by St. Thomas in the passage quoted above, and perhaps it ought not to be attributed to him at all. And yet, I think it is certainly not alien to his general notion of logic, and it may be actually implied by it. Briefly, I might formulate this second criterion of intentionality thus: logical intentions, in addition to being *consequent* upon reason's consideration of the things of nature, are also *instrumental* to reason's consideration of things. In other words, logical intentions are the tools and means of human knowledge, quite as much as they are the products of such knowledge —or better, they are produced in the process of knowledge, precisely in order that through them such knowledge may be made possible.

For instance, to take our earlier example of hydrogen, it is certainly true that in the process of coming to know that hydrogen is an element, that it has such and such an atomic weight, etc., we treat hydrogen as being the species of a genus and make it the subject of a proposition. In itself, hydrogen is neither a species nor a subject, but in its condition of being known and as an object before the mind, it takes on these purely logical features or "intentions," as they are called. At the same time, must it not also be recognized that the reason hydrogen thus comes to be placed in the purely logical relationships of being a species of a genus or a subject of a predicate is precisely in order that we may thereby come to know that hydrogen really is an element or that

it does in fact have an atomic weight
of 1.008?

Moreover, if logical entities and relations may be said to be "intentional," not
merely in the sense of being objects of
second intention, as the Scholastics would
say, but also in the sense of being the
necessary instruments of any and all
ordinary human cognitive intentions,[17]
then presumably these logical intentions
must needs have a character that fits
them for the peculiar intentional functions
which they are supposed to perform precisely as such instruments of cognition.
And so, it seems to me, they do have.
Specifically, I would suggest that all of
the main instruments of traditional logic
—concepts,[18] propositions, and arguments
—are, in form and structure, simply relations of identity. Moreover, it is just this
kind of a structure which enables them to
function intentionally in the way just
described.

For instance, to take just one illustration, that of the affirmative categorical proposition, do we not think of the P term as being related to the S, precisely in the sense that 'P' represents what S is? And yet what is such a relation of a thing to what it is—to its own 'what'—if not a relation of identity? Moreover, it should be remarked that in fact and in reality nothing ever stands over against its own 'what' in such a way as to be related back to it by a relation of identity, in the manner of predicate to subject. No, it is only intellectually or in the mind that what-a-thing-is is abstracted from the thing itself and then reidentified[19] with it in a logical proposition.

And yet note that through the device of such a purely logical relating of a thing to its own 'what', we do come to recognize what that thing is in fact and in reality. Nor would it seem that there was any other way whereby we could come to know what a thing is save through thus setting the thing, so to speak, over against its own 'what' and then relating the two by a relation of identity. In other words, the relation of identity that the mind sets up between subject and predicate in a proposition is an intentional relation precisely in the sense that through it the mind or reason is able to intend things as they are in themselves and in reality. *What* thus comes to be intended is not a relation of identity; but *that through which* it is intended is a relation of identity.

And now let us return to a consideration of Frege's schema of function and argument, which, as we have seen, is the basic ordering principle for the whole of modern logic and which, if I am right, might be said to play a role in the new logic not unlike that of the relation of identity in traditional logic. Very well, can it be said that this basic schema or pattern of function and argument is an "intentional" one, in the same sense in which we have suggested that the relation of identity is an intentional relation? The answer, I think, must be decisively, "No."

In support of this, let me adduce two considerations. In the first place, it is apparent that the relation of a function to its argument or arguments is not a relation of identity, and that in consequence the function can in no sense be regarded as representing what the argument or arguments are. Thus to take Frege's own example of the function '$2.(\ )^3+(\ )$', this could hardly be regarded as representing what any possible argument of the function—say the number 4—is. Likewise, if the function be a relation and the arguments of the function the things so related, clearly the former could hardly be regarded as representing or signifying what the latter are. For example, in the proposition 'Milwaukee is north of Chicago,' 'north of' is the function and 'Chicago' and 'Milwaukee' are the arguments of the function. And yet surely, no one would suppose that 'being north of' signifies what Milwaukee and Chicago conjointly are, in the same way in which 'being an element' signifies what hydrogen is.

Moreover, as a second consideration in support of my contention that the schema of function and argument is not an intentional schema at all, I might merely point out that, unlike the relation of identity between subject and predicate, the relation between argument and function is not one whose nature is simply to be of or about something else. And the reason is that by Frege's own account[20] a function is understood as being simply the order of parts in a whole. That is why, as we saw from our earlier quotation from Frege, a function just in itself is incomplete or unsaturated and why, as he says, the function must go together with the arguments "to make up a complete whole." But a complete whole of this sort is not a mere being of reason, nor is it an instrument for the intention of something other than itself. Thus the ordered whole of Milwaukee-north-of-Chicago is not of or about anything else after the manner of a logical intention. On the contrary, the spatial order that Milwaukee stands in with respect to Chicago is itself the real order of things. It is in no sense a being of reason which serves as an instrument for intending the real as other and different from itself.

But now having considered in some detail just what the function-argument schema of modern logic is, as well as how and in what sense this schema may be said to lack intentionality in the traditional sense, it remains for us to look briefly into the current controversy in semantics between realists and nominalists. For if I am right in my contention, this controversy is rather directly traceable to the use in modern logic of Frege's function-argument schema. Moreover, it is because this schema is a non-intentional one that its use in logic tends to render the issue be-

tween realism and nominalism at once
inevitable and insoluable—or at least so it
would seem to me.

To return again, then, to Bertrand
Russell. As everyone knows, in his earliest
logical writings he tended to adopt a very
extreme realistic position. Nor is it sur-
prising that he should have done so. For
having adopted Frege's schema, Russell
supposed that any and every proposition
could be analyzed into a function and one
or more arguments. Moreover, so far as
so-called first level, atomic propositions[21]
were concerned, Russell felt that the argument signs stood for ultimate and irreducible particulars, whereas the function
signs stood for universals or relations.[22]
For instance, in the proposition 'Socrates
was an Athenian,' 'Socrates' is the argument and is particular,[23] whereas 'being
an Athenian' is the function and is universal. Or again, in the proposition,
'Socrates was older than Plato', 'Socrates'
and 'Plato' are the arguments and are, of

course, particulars, whereas 'being older than' is the function and is a relation or universal.

Not only that, but we are all familiar with how propositions, which from the point of view of traditional logic would seem to involve universals as subjects or arguments, are in the new logic subjected to a further analysis, which simply relegates all elements of universality to the role of predicates or functions, leaving only particulars in the position of arguments. For instance, if we take Aristotle's celebrated proposition, 'All ruminants part the hoof,' Russell and all other mathematical logicians would render this,[24] 'For any x, if x is a ruminant, x parts the hoof.' Or again, a particular proposition like 'Some lectures are dull' becomes a conjunction: 'There is at least one x, such that x is a lecture and x is dull.' In other words, by virtue of such analyses the ordinary atomic proposition of the first level may be shown to have only particulars for its arguments, whereas all relations, as well as all universals, must be regarded as pertaining to the function side of the schema. But now if logical propositions are thus analyzed in terms of functions and their arguments, and if the arguments are identified with particulars, and functions with universals, then what about the semantics of propositions so understood? That is to say, just what is it that a proposition compounded out of a function and its argument or arguments may be said to mean or signify? Already the answer to this semantic question would seem predetermined by the very nature of the case. For a function-argument structure, as we have seen, is not an intentional one. In this respect it is quite unlike a purely intentional relation of identity such as that of subject to predicate. Thus the latter sort of relation is such that it can be used to intend something other and different from itself. For instance, in our earlier example of hydrogen having an atomic weight of 1.008, we made 'hydro-gen' the subject and we predicated 'having an atomic weight of 1.008' of it. However, in thus *using* a relation of identity between subject and predicate, we did not *mean* or *intend* by it any real relation of identity in fact and in reality. For *in rerum natura* hydrogen is not related to its atomic weight by any identity relation of subject to predicate.

However, if a function - argument structure does not have this sort of inten-tional relationship toward something other than itself, which it is supposed somehow to be of or about, then just how is a proposition which is interpreted as having this kind of structure related to what it means or signifies? Russell's answer to this question—at least in his earlier writings—was that the relation of a proposition to the fact which it means or signifies is simply a relation of corres-pondence.[25]

"In a logically correct symbolism," he

remarks, "there will always be a certain fundamental identity of structure between a fact and the symbol for it; and . . . the complexity of the symbol corresponds very closely with the complexity of the facts symbolized by it . . . it is quite directly evident to inspection that the fact, for example, that two things stand in a certain relation to one another—e.g., that this is to the left of that—is itself objectively complex, and not merely that the apprehension of it is complex. The fact that two things stand in a certain relation to each other, or any statement of this sort, has a complexity all of its own. I shall therefore in future assume that there is an objective complexity in the world, and that it is mirrored by the complexity of propositions."[26]

In other words, for Russell those parts of a proposition which are called arguments stand for or signify particulars or individuals, and that part of the proposition which is called the function corresponds to or signifies a real universal or relation *in rerum natura.* Or as he himself puts it in another connection:

The reason that I call my doctrine

> *logical* atomism is because the atoms that .
> I wish to arrive at as a sort of last residue
> in analysis are logical atoms . . . Some of
> them will be what I call "particulars,"—
> such things as little patches of color or
> sounds, momentary things—and some of
> them will be predicates or relations and
> so on. The point is that the atom I wish
> to arrive at is the atom of logical an-
> alysis . . .[27]

Here, certainly, we have a most extreme realism, even if a somewhat curious
and bizarre one. For universals are not
only held to be real on this view; in addition, they are said to be like so many atoms
existing outside of and along side of particulars. Nor would there seem to be much
doubt that it was simply on the basis of
his analysis of the proposition into logical
atoms of argument and function that
Russell was led to believe that there must
correspond to these in reality, the real
atoms of particulars and universals. A
strange view, indeed. However, it did not
prove to be a view of very long duration.

As a matter of fact, from even a very

cursory knowledge of the history of philosophy, one might be led to suspect that, whether it be the realism of a William of Champeaux or that of a Bertrand Russell, no sooner would such a realism make its appearance than its nominalistic antithesis would not be far behind. As a matter of fact, in Russell's case it was he himself who early began to have doubts about the tenability of his own realism. And the source of these doubts presumably lay in such seemingly innocuous little words as 'or,' 'if-then,' 'and' etc. Thus Russell describes his misgivings in this way:

> Are there logical constants? There is one sense of this question in which we can give a perfectly definite affirmative answer: in the linguistic or symbolic expression of logical propositions, there are words or symbols which play a constant part, i.e., make the same contribution to the significance of propositions wherever they occur. Such are, for example, "or," "and," "not," "if-then," "the null-class," "0," "1," "2" . . . The difficulty is that,

when we analyze the propositions in the written expression of which such symbols occur, we find that they have no constituents corresponding to the expressions in question. In some cases this is fairly obvious: not even the most ardent Platonist would suppose that the perfect "or" is laid up in heaven, and that the "or's" here on earth are imperfect copies of the celestial archtype. But in the case of numbers this is far less obvious ... At the time when I wrote the "Principles," I shared with Frege a belief in the Platonic reality of numbers, which, in my imagination, peopled the timeless realm of Being. It was a comforting faith, which I later abandoned with regret. Something must now be said of the steps by which I was led to abandon it.

In Chap. IV of the "Principles" it is said that "every word occurring in a sentence must have some meaning;" and again, "Whatever may be an object of thought, or may occur in any true or false proposition, or can be counted as one, I call a term. . . . A man, a moment, a number, a class, a relation, a chimaera, or anything else that can be mentioned, is sure to be a term; and to deny that such and such a thing is a term must always be false." This way of understanding language turned out to be mistaken. That a word "must have some meaning"—the word, of course, being not gibberish, but one which has an intelligible use—is not always true if taken as applying to the word in isolation. What is true is that the word contributes to the meaning of the sentence in which it occurs; but that is a very different matter.

Logical constants, therefore, if we are to be able to say anything definite about them, must be treated as part of the language, not as part of what the language speaks about. In this way, logic becomes much more linguistic than I believed it to be at the time when I wrote the "Principles." It will still be true that no constants except logical constants occur in the verbal or symbolic expression of logical propositions, but it will not be true that these logical constants are names or objects, as "Socrates" is intended to be.[28]

Such admissions, it is true, do not constitute as yet any profession of faith in extreme nominalism; still they do represent a considerable departure from extreme realism. And as a matter of fact,

for a number of years following the
original impact of the new logic most
logicians and semanticists might be said
to have tried to maintain themselves in a
sort of half-way house between realism
and nominalism. Thus their common
practise was to distinguish sharply between what they called the "logical words"
of a language on the one hand the "descriptive words" on the other.[29] The
former were supposed to correspond
roughly to what the Scholastics had
called syncategorematic terms, and the
latter to categorematic terms. Conse-
quently, while it was thought that the
latter sort of terms or words actually sig-
nified real things, the former sort—words
such as 'or,' 'if-then,' 'the,' 'some' etc.—
quite obviously did not.

But unfortunately, if the framework of
one's logic is Frege's schema of function
and argument, it becomes exceedingly
difficult to remain in this half-way house
between realism and nominalism. For

after all, 'if-then,' 'or' and 'the' are just as much function terms as are 'hydrogen,' 'heavier than,' and 'yellow.' Hence, if in attempting to give a semantic interpretation of one's logical structures, one insists that there is something *in rerum natura* corresponding to the latter sort of term, but not to the former, one's whole procedure would appear to be a very arbitrary one indeed. Either all function terms, it would seem, would have something corresponding to them in fact, or none of them would. There just is no half-way house.

Moreover, if I understand him, this is precisely what Professor Quine of Harvard is currently engaged in doing: he is attacking the half-way house between realism and nominalism and is insisting that one ought to go all the way in the direction of nominalism.[30] For him, in short, no function term should be interpreted as meaning or designating anything real at all.[31] Nor according to him can the

distinction any longer be maintained between "logical" words and "descriptive"
words, or syncategorematic terms and
categorematic terms. For just as many of
us might suppose that 'or' or 'although' or
'the' do not refer to any real entities corresponding to these terms, so Quine would
be equally insistent that there is no such
thing as redness to which the term 'red'
might be thought to refer, or no real relation of equality which a propositional
function like 'equal to' might be supposed
to intend or signify.

Indeed, Professor Quine does not confine himself to cases like 'or,' 'although'
and 'the,' when he wants to give examples
of syncategorematic expressions. No, he
even mentions such things as the word
'up' or the suffix 'ness' or signs of punctuation.[32] These are obviously syncategorematic. That is to say, they are quite
meaningful in the contexts of the sentences
in which they appear; and yet, though
meaningful, they are certainly not used to

designate or refer to any real entities corresponding to them.[33]

But then ordinary nouns and adjectives, which most of us would suppose were unmistakeably categorematic, Professor Quine would say, are no more categorematic than 'up' or the suffix 'ness.' Thus as he remarks,

> . . . There is no such thing as *up*. In repudiating an entity *"up"* we do not change our views as to the truth or falsehood of any ordinary factual statement containing the word "up." But we do claim that nothing, neither a spatiotemporal body nor even a property or other abstract entity, is *designated* by the word "up;" the word is meaningful, it forms an essential part of various statements, but it is not a noun, much less a name of anything.
>
> Now the nominalist goes one step further in his repudiation of abstract entities. He would say, in the same spirit in which we have repudiated *up*, that there is no such thing as appendicitis. The word "appendicitis" is meaningful and useful in context; yet he can maintain that the word is not a *name* of an entity in its own right,

and that it is a noun at all only because of a regrettable strain of realism which pervades our own particular language. . . . The general term "horse" will fare no better; there are many denoted entities in this case, indeed—many horses[34] but no *named* or designated entity, no abstract property *horse* according to the nominalist.[35]

Indeed, one might say that it is a part of the avowed program of a nominalist logician like Quine to shift all categorematic words into the class of the syncategorematic and to handle all "descriptive" words as if they were ultimately and in principle no different from "logical" words.

There is no doubt about it: this certainly sounds like nominalism all right. And as such, it would appear to be at the very opposite extreme from the so-called platonic realism of Frege and the early Russell. Not only that, but it has also left far behind the half-way house of those who would maintain that whereas certain function words of the basic function-argument schema—*viz.* the syncategorematic words—do not name or designate any real entities corresponding to them, all the other function words—*viz.* the categorematic ones—do.

Nevertheless, our purpose is not merely to confirm the fact that the function-argument schema has indeed given rise to an extreme nominalistic type of semantics. More particularly, our concern is to see just how such a nominalism was generated out of such a schema.

Already in considering how this schema lent itself to an extreme realistic interpretation, we noted that in its actual employment by Russell as a schema for first-level atomic propositions, the effect of the schema was to relegate all universality to the function pole and to confine particularity simply to the argument pole. Not only that, but since the relation of argument to function is not a relation of identity after the manner of the traditional

subject-predicate relation, one cannot consider that the function in any sense represents what the argument or arguments are.
On the contrary, function and argument
are ranged over against one another in a
kind of atom-like independence, with the
result that the only proper arguments for
propositional functions must needs be the
barest of bare particulars. Indeed, no
sooner do any of these bare particulars
display so much as a shred of character
than all such characterizing features are
immediately stripped off of them, and
relegated to the function pole of the
proposition. And on Russell's theory of
logical atomism that which corresponds in
reality to the function pole of the proposition is a very different kind of entity from
the sort of thing that corresponds to the
argument pole. The former is a real
atomic universal or relation; the latter a
real particular that is as bare as bare
can be.

Now all this is quite to the taste of the

nominalist, if only he can find some ground for denying that real universals correspond to the function side of propositions, while continuing to affirm that real, and yet utterly bare, particulars correspond to the argument side. And such a ground Professor Quine thinks he has found in his so-called theory of reference, or better in his theory of the distinction of reference from meaning.[36] Moreover, the significant thing about this theory of reference is that it seems to be demanded by the very exigencies of the function-argument schema itself. In fact, it was Russell himself who originally enunciated the theory, even though he seems not to have recognized its nominalistic import.

Briefly, what this theory of reference comes down to is simply this. It states that in any proposition involving a function-argument structure, while both parts of the proposition may be presumed to be meaningful and significant, still in asserting the proposition as a whole, what one asserts to exist are only the arguments and not the function. Nor is it either without interest or without relevance for us to consider how Russell was led to this theory.[37]

Its origin may be traced to Russell's embarrassment over what we might paradoxically term unreal entities—things like sea-serpents, the present King of France, square-circles, etc. For Russell was convinced that anything that a proposition might be said to be about—i.e., the argument or arguments of the propositional function—would necessarily have to be or to exist in order for the proposition to be about them. But then how could a proposition be about the present King of France, say, if there were no such person? Or again, what is one to do about a proposition like 'Sea-serpents do not exist'? Must one somehow suppose that there are sea-serpents and that they do exist, in order to be able to assert that they do not exist?

Now in order to get around such fancied difficulties as these, Russell insisted that these propositions, although they might seem to be about such things as sea-serpents and the present King of France are really not so at all. And the reason is that sea-serpents, the present King of France, etc., really aren't proper arguments of propositional functions. Instead, they contain descriptive elements in them, just as much as do terms like 'human being,' 'hydrogen,' 'ruminants,' etc. Accordingly, just as in the latter case we saw how all descriptive elements must be analyzed out of the argument pole and relegated to the function pole, so also the same thing must be done in the former case too. Thus the real forms of such propositions would be something like this:

> 'There is an x, such that x is King of France and is bald, and nothing else is King of France.'
> 'There is an x, such that x is a sea-serpent and x lives in the sea.'

On such an analysis, then, the proposition is seen not to be about a King of France who doesn't exist or about a sea-serpent which is simply a non-being. No, it's about nothing more than an x or a bare something.[38] And if it's false that any such x is a sea-serpent or a square circle or what not, then the proposition as a whole is false. And yet this does not mean that there must be a sea-serpent in order for us to say that there is not one, or that there must be a present King of France in order for us to repudiate the proposition that he is bald.

But right here, Professor Quine thinks he finds all that he needs to substantiate his nominalism. For not only does the analysis of a proposition into a function and its arguments tend to distinguish bare particulars from all descriptive attributes, but in addition the assertion of the proposition commits one only to the assertion of the existence of such bare particulars or mere x's, and not at all to the assertion of any descriptive attributes.[39] To be sure, the function elements in propositions to which such descriptions are relegated are meaningful and significant; and yet that does not mean that they refer to or designate any real entities corresponding to them. Indeed, its the same as with function signs like 'if' and 'or'. These are certainly meaningful and significant in context; and yet we don't for a minute suppose on this account that they actually name or refer to little existing 'if's' and 'or's' *in rerum natura.*

But at this point you may well protest and say, "Surely, this can't be. It's too utterly fantastic. For how can Professor Quine maintain a position such as this? Function terms like 'red,' 'tree,' 'equal to,' 'brother of,' etc., are said to designate nothing in reality at all—i.e., there just is no redness, no substantial nature of trees, no relations of equality or of brotherhood, which these function terms might be said to mean or signify. On the other hand, as to the argument variables, while it is true that when these are quantified, they are supposed to designate real existent entities, still what are the entities so designated? Apparently they are nothing but bare x's, mere something's.[40] But as to what sorts of things they are or as to what their natures are, we cannot properly say, since no function term designates a real 'what' of anything. Indeed, not only can we not say what they are; in addition it would seem that these bare x's cannot even be what they are. For there just are no real 'what's' or natures that they could in any wise be or have. *What* are they then? Apparently, not anything. But this is just preposterous!"

Very well, make such protests if you will. Yet what I should here like to stress is not so much the strange and even preposterous character of such nominalism, but rather the fact that this curious sort of nominalism, along with its equally curious realistic predecessor, should loom up in modern semantics as alternatives that are seemingly so ineluctable and yet really so unnecessary.

That they should seem so ineluctable becomes readily understandable, once one tries to do logic using a radically nonintentional schema like that of function and argument. For on the grounds of such a schema it is utterly inconceivable how logical entities and devices like 'if-then' conjunctions, logical universals, subjects-predicates, etc., can be of such a nature as to enable us through them to come to intend and know entities and structures in reality which may well be other and different from the logical devices through which they have thus come to be intended and known. And being unable to recognize this intentional character of logical entities, modern logicians and semanticists have found themselves forced into one or the other of two very embarrassing alternatives. Either the non-intentional logical schema of function and argument may be presumed to have real entitites corresponding to each of its two poles, in which case the logician-semanticist finds himself committed to a rather strange and wondrous realism. Or this same non-intentional schema may be presumed to have nothing corresponding to its respective elements—or at least not to its function element—in which case the use of the function-argument schema will involve no more than a vague reference to the real, a reference which turns out to be no more than a mere naming or designating of bare x's, something's, anything's.

But having said this much, have we not already said enough to indicate that this whole dispute in contemporary semantics, while unavoidable against the background of modern logic, is really quite unnecessary? For the entire trouble would seem to stem from the use in modern logic of a schema like that of function and argument, which turns out to be radically non-intentional, and hence not adapted to the proper purposes of logic at all.

In contrast, a genuine logical intention, as we remarked before, not only is a mere being of reason and hence not a form or schema for real relationships at all; but in addition, as an instrument of knowledge, it will have a nature or character such that through the use of it, *viz*. the intention, one can thereby come to know something other and different from it, *viz*. the object intended.[41]

Once such a principle of intentionality is recognized, one is no longer, it would seem, faced with quite the realistic-nominalistic difficulties that so perplex modern semanticists. Thus merely because one uses a universal concept as one's logical instrument, certainly does not imply that one means or signifies by it a real universal entity existing extra-mentally, as the realists would seem to hold;[42] nor is the only alternative to this the nominalistic one of supposing that in using a universal concept, one does not thereby mean or signify anything real at all.

Or again, if we suppose that the relation between subject and predicate in a proposition be an intentional relation of identity, then clearly in using such a proposition, we do not thereby intend any real relation of identity existing *in rerum natura*. For instance, the assertion that many Wisconsin barns are red certainly is not to be taken as signifying that there are a number of barns in Wisconsin that actually and in fact stand in a relation of identity to the red color they happen to be painted. But on the other hand and equally, merely because in using an intentional relation of identity we do not thereby mean or intend any real relation of identity existing in nature, that certainly does not force us to accept the embarrassing alternative of supposing that by such a relation we do not mean or signify anything real at all. Quite the contrary, we can perfectly legitimately consider that a purely logical relation of identity between a subject term like 'barns' and a predicate term 'red' is the means or instrument whereby we intend a real relation of substance to accident *in rerum natura*[43]— a relation which quite patently is not a relation of identity at all.

Nor do the "logical connectives" or syncategorematic words that have given modern semanticists so much trouble— words like 'if-then,' 'or,' 'and,' etc.—need be a source of trouble either, if only they be understood as logical intentions, rather than as Fregean functions.[44] Thus, for instance, in using a propositional connection of the sort expressed by the English words, 'if-then', we certainly do not thereby intend or signify a real 'if' existing *in rerum natura.* And yet surely we do wish to intend or signify something in reality by such a logical relating of antecedent to consequent.[45] What is it then? Well, my suggestion would be that through such a purely logical relation of dependence of consequent upon antecedent, we ordinarily mean to signify some such thing as a real cause-effect dependence in reality.[46]

Moreover, what would be true of that logical relation between propositions that is expressed by an 'if-then' conjunction would also be true, *mutatis mutandis,* of such other logical relations as are expressed by other conjunctions—e.g., 'or,' 'and,' 'although,' 'because,' etc. In each case, if the relation be taken as an intention, then so far from having to suppose that the logical relation must either correspond to a similar relation in reality or else signify nothing in reality at all, we may rather consider that through the instrument of such intentional relations we are brought to a recognition of other and different relations in reality.[47]

Let this then suffice by way of a brief account of the principle of intentionality in logic and the unhappy consequences of its almost complete neglect by contemporary realists and nominalists alike. Perhaps in conclusion, I could do no better than call attention to an almost lapidary formulation of this principle by St. Thomas

Aquinas. In the second book of the
Summa contra Gentiles, chapter 75, St.
Thomas has just observed that merely
because all the sciences have to do with
universals, that certainly does not mean
that universals must subsist in themselves
and outside the mind, as Plato had supposed.[48] There then follows the reason:

> For although it be necessary for the
> truth of a cognition that the cognition
> answer to the thing known, still it is not
> necessary that the mode of the thing
> known be the same as the mode of its
> cognition.[49]

Somehow, one wonders whether, if
only this simple and rather obvious principle of intentionality had been observed
by modern logicians, there would ever
have been the current and seemingly futile
dispute between realists and nominalists
among modern semanticists. Once again,
we would seem to be forcibly reminded of
the truth that there is such a thing as the
"unity of philosophical experience."

Notes

1. V. *The Unity of Philosophical Experience,*
Chapter I. Charles Scribner's Sons, New York,
1937.

2. *Ibid.,* pp. 6-12.

3. Cf. the statement of W. V. Quine in his essay
entitled, "On What There is": ". . . the modern
philosophical mathematicians have not on the
whole recognized that they were debating the
same old problem of universals in a newly
clarified form. . . . The three main medieval
points of view regarding universals are designated by historians as *realism, conceptualism,*
and *nominalism.* Essentially these same three
doctrines reappear in twentieth century sur-
veys of the philosophy of mathematics under
the new names *logicism, intuitionism,* and
formalism." From a Logical Point of View.
Harvard University Press, Cambridge, 1953,
p. 14.

4. It is true that many contemporary Oxford
and Cambridge philosophers who are partisans
of so-called "ordinary language" would no

doubt consider themselves nominalists in matters of semantics and yet at the same time would tend more or less to disparge modern formal logic. Notwithstanding this, I rather imagine that these latter-day lovers of ordinary language—though not of extraordinary logic—would still exemplify the sort of thing Gilson would mean by "logicism" in philosophy.

5. This is what contemporary nominalists delight in dubbing their realist opponents. (V. Quine, "On Universals," *Journal of Symbolic Logic*, 12, No. 3, September, 1947, p. 74). Since it is presumabley meant as a term of opprobrium, the so-called realists who are the beneficiaries of the epithet seem generally not to like it. (Cf. Carnap, "Empiricism, Semantics, and Ontology," *Revue Internationale de Philosophie*, 11 (1950), p. 34).

6. I should perhaps explain that I am using the word "schema" in roughly the same sense as Professor W. V. Quine when he says, "Schemata are logical diagrams of statements." (V. *Methods of Logic*, Henry Holt and Co., New York, 1950, p. 22. Also *passim*). Needless to say, this use of the term should not be confused with the Kantian sense of "schema" which

Professor C. I. Lewis has sometimes made use of. (Cf. his *An Analysis of Knowledge and Valuation,* The Open Court Publishing Co., La Salle, Illinois, 1946, pp. 134 ff.)

7. *Translations from the Philosophical Writings of Gottlob Frege,* edited by Peter Geach and Max Black. Philosophical Library, New York, 1952, p. 24.

8. *Ibid.,* pp. 24-25.

9. *Ibid.,* p. 31.

10. These two ways of turning a propositional function into a proposition might be illustrated roughly as follows. Take the function, 'x is tall.' This may be turned into a proposition either by giving a specific value to the variable—e.g., 'John is tall,' or by quantifying the variable. For example, by universal quantification one would get 'Everything is tall'

or

'(x).x is tall.'

Or, by particular or existential quantification one would get

'At least one thing is tall'

or

'(x).x is tall.'

11. *Our Knowledge of the External World,* first

published 1914, reissued by George Allen and Unwin, Ltd., London, 1922, p. 56. Cf. also p 54.

12.   *Ibid.*, pp. 18-19.

13.   *Mysticism and Logic,* p. 112. Quoted in Charles H. Fritz, Jr., *Bertrand Russell's Construction of the External World,* New York and London, 1952, p. 203.

14.   S. Thomae Aquinatis, *In Metaphysicam Aristotelis Commentaria,* ed. by Cathala, Turin, 1935. Sec. 574. Since my translation is rather free, I append the text: "Ens autem rationis dicitur proprie de illis intentionibus, quas ratio adinvenit in rebus consideratis; sicut intentio generis, speciei et similium, quae quidem non inveniuntur in rerum natura, sed considerationem rationis consequuntur. Et huiusmodi, scilicet ens rationis, est proprie subjectum logicae."

15.   In my efforts to gain something like a right understanding of St. Thomas' specifically logical doctrines, I have been greatly aided by discussion with Rev. Robert W. Schmidt, S.J., of West Baden College, as well as by a reading of his excellent book, *The Domain of Logic According to St. Thomas Aquinas,* (Doctoral

dissertation, University of Toronto, 1947). At the same time, Father Schmidt must not be held responsible for any of the views expressed in this lecture.

16.   Father Schmidt has suggested to me that a better rendering of *adinvenit* might be 'devise,' 'contrive,' or 'elaborate.' Cf. his *The Domain of Logic, op. cit.*, p. 185.

17.   Needless to say, it is not implied that these two senses of intentionality are either incompatible or unrelated. On the contrary, the logical entities and relations that are made the objects of second intention are themselves in a sense the means and instruments of first intention.

18.   Father Schmidt suggests that logic is properly concerned only with the reflex and not with the direct concept. *Op. cit.*, p. 144.

19.   Perhaps the term 're-identified' is misleading, since it is not to be supposed that there exists an original real relation of identity between a thing and its 'what,' which is first destroyed in the act of abstraction and then restored in the act of judgment. Nevertheless, if the term 're-identified' is not thus taken too

literally, it should not be misleading but rather suggestive.

In this connection there is an interesting passage in Sec. 216, Part I of Wittgenstein's recently published *Philosophical Investigations* (The Macmillan Co., New York, 1953):

"A thing is identical with itself."—There is no finer example of a useless proposition, which yet is connected with a certain play of the imagination. It is as if in imagination we put a thing into its own shape and saw that it fitted.

20.   V. the quotation given on p. 3, *supra.*

21.   An atomic proposition may be understood as a simple proposition which is made up of terms and relations (or qualities), and hence is not compounded of other proposittions. In contrast, a molecular proposition is compounded of atomic propositions joined by connectives like 'or,' 'if-then,' etc. Cf. *Our Knowledge of the External World,* pp. 62 ff. *The Philosophy of Logical Atomism,* Department of Philosophy, University of Minnesota, n.d., pp. 17 ff. Also, Fritz, *op. cit.,* pp. 121 ff.

By first level propositions are to be understood propositions of the lowest logical type. Thus on the theory of types no propositional function can be its own argument. Hence propositions on the lowest level will have ultimate particulars or individuals as their arguments, on the second level the arguments will be the first level functions, on the third level they will be the functions of functions, etc. To be sure, this is a somewhat overly simple statement of the matter. For the full account, v. Whitehead and Russell, *Principia Mathematica*, 2nd edition, Cambridge, at the University Press, 1950, Vol. I, Introduction, Ch. II.

22. For a brief and lucid account of this view of Russell's, v. Fritz, *op. cit.*, pp. 117 ff.

23. It is true that Russell would not consider that Socrates was properly an "ultimate simple" or irreducible particular. Cf. Fritz, *op. cit.*, pp. 124-125. Also, *The Philosophy of Logical Atomism*, Chapter II, pp. 8 ff.

24. For a brief statement by Russell himself of this way of interpreting the universal and particular propositions of traditional logic. v. *Introduction to Mathematical Philosophy*, 2nd edition, George Allen and Unwin, Ltd., London, 1920, pp. 161-165.

25. *Cf.* Fritz, *op. cit.*, p. 126: "The correspondence between propositions and facts might

lead one to assume that Russell favors a correspondence theory of truth, and such an assumption I believe is correct."

26. *The Philosophy of Logical Atomism,* pp. 12-13.

27. *Ibid.,* p. 1.

28. *The Principles of Mathematics,* 2nd edition, W. W. Norton and Company, Inc., New York, 1937, pp. IX-X.

29. *Cf.* Carnap, R., *Foundation of Logic and Mathematics,* in the *International Encyclopedia of Unified Science,* Vol. 1, No. 3, University of Chicago Press, 1939, p. 7: "We divide the signs . . . into two classes: *descriptive* and *logical* signs. As descriptive signs we take those which designate things or properties of things (in a more comprehensive system we should classify here also the relations among things, functions of things, etc.). The other signs are taken as logical signs: they serve chiefly for connecting descriptive signs in the construction of sentences but do not themselves designate things, properties of things, etc. Logical signs are, e.g., those corresponding to English words like 'is,' 'are,' 'not,' 'and,' 'or,' 'if,' 'any,' 'some,' 'every,' 'all.' "

30. Unfortunately, the term "nominalism" is very imprecise, covering a great multitude of rather different philosophic sins and perhaps even a few philosophic virtues. Nor in this brief essay do I propose to fix the meaning of the term so that one will be able to determine in the case of a given nominalist in just what sense he is a nominalist.

Nevertheless, it might be well to make a little clearer just which aspects of Professor Quine's nominalism will here be under examination. To begin with, let us note how Quine himself would contrast his own position with that of the "platonists": "Where the *platonists* (as I shall call those who accept universals) differ from their opponents, the *nominalists,* is in positing a realm of entities, universals, corresponding to such general or abstract words. . . .

"The platonist is likely to regard the word 'man' as naming a universal, the class of men or the property of being a man, much as the word 'Caesar' names the concrete object Caesar."

("On Universals," *Journal of Symbolic Logic,* 12, No. 3, Sept., 1947, p. 74).

Now if one wishes to follow the more or

less standard way of distinguishing between realists, conceptualists, and nominalists, that is adopted, for example, by R. I. Aaron (*The Theory of Universals*, Clarendon Press, Oxford, 1952), then one would need to say that the statement just quoted from Quine, in which he attempts to distinguish nominalism from platonism, is still not sufficient to distinguish nominalism from conceptualism. To this end one must, according to Aaron, go farther and recognize that "the distinction between conceptualist and nominalist must lie finally in this, that the former asserts the existence of a concept along with the name, whereas the latter denies the need for the concept and holds that the universal is merely the name." (*Ibid.*, p. 20.)

Now it seems to me that by this criterion Quine would be not just a conceptualist, but a nominalist. Indeed, this, I take it, is the thrust of his greatly self-advertised criterion of ontological commitment, "To be is to be the value of a variable." (V. the essay "On What There Is" in *From a Logical Point of View*, Harvard University Press, Cambridge, 1953, esp. p. 15), together with his repeated efforts to carry through his program for constructing an ade-

quate language in which it will not be necessary for function terms ever to be the arguments of further functions (*Cf. ibid.*, essay VI,
"Logic and the Reification of Universals").

Be it noted, however, that in this present
essay, we shall at no time be concerned with
this latter aspect of Quine's nominalism. Instead, our concern will be simply with the
nominalist's denial of universals considered as
extra-mental entities, corresponding to the
function terms of logical propositions. In this
respect, the further means of differentiating
nominalists from conceptualists, as suggested
by Aaron, for example, will be irrelevant to our
purpose.

31.   One might suppose that this is unfair to
Quine. For one thing, he repeatedly insists that
universal words, and function words generally,
while they do not mean or signify any universal things or entities, are nevertheless meaningful and significant in context. (*Cf.* "On Universals," *op. cit.*, p. 74; also "Designation and
Existence," *Readings in Philosophical Analysis,*
edited by Feigl and Sellars, Appleton-Century-
Crofts, Inc., New York, 1949, pp. 44-51,
passim).

Nevertheless, when one begins to ask just

what it is that these meaningful and significant function terms mean and signify, then Quine's answers, it seems to me, though exceedingly voluble, are neither very clear nor altogether consistent.

Thus one line that he appears to take is that a function term or word may perfectly well mean or signify other words or other expressions in the language, but without its thereby naming or designating anything real or extra-linguistic. Now this is based on Quine's well-known distinction of what he calls the theory of reference or naming from the theory of meaning. (V. "On What There Is," esp. pp. 5-9. Also, "Two Dogmas of Empiricism," in *From a Logical Point of View*, p. 22). More-over, once this distinction is recognized, the way is opened for Quine to treat all categore-matic terms (universals and relations) as if they were syncategorematic. 'Man,' 'red,' 'horse,' 'ancestor of,' are just like 'up,' the suf-fix '-ness' and logical connectives such as 'or,' 'if,' 'and,' etc.—all of them alike are meaning-ful in context, but designate nothing in reality. (*Cf.* "Designation and Existence," pp. 45-47 and 50-51). On this basis, therefore, the state-ment made in the text above that "no function term should be interpreted as meaning or des-

ignating anything real at all" is entirely justi-
fied.

Nevertheless, this is not the only line which
Quine's nominalism follows with respect to the
meaning and significance of function terms.
For like so many nominalists, Quine at times
speaks very disarmingly and in a vein that
many a moderate realist must needs feel very
sympathetic with. Thus consider the following passage: "One may admit that there are
real houses, roses, and sunsets, but deny, except as a popular and misleading manner of
speaking, that they have anything in common.
The words 'houses,' 'roses,' and 'sunsets' are
true of sundry individual entities which are
houses, and roses, and sunsets, and the word
'red' or 'red object' is true of each of sundry individual entities which are red houses, red
roses, red sunsets; but there is not, in addition,
any entity whatever, individual or otherwise,
which is named by the word 'redness,' nor, for
that matter, by the word 'household,' 'rose-
hood,' or 'sunsethood.'" ("On What There Is,"
p. 10.)

Now as an interpretation of nominalism,
this may be all very well, and yet it is difficult
to see just how it is consistent with the other

sort of interpretation which Quine places upon his nominalism. For if 'red,' 'houses,' and 'roses' may designate and be true of sundry real individual entities, then Quine cannot consistently say that universals do not mean or designate any real, extra-linguistic entities at all. Or *vice versa*, if Quine wishes to hold that terms such as 'red,' 'houses,' and 'roses' are altogether on a par with wholly syncategorematic elements like the suffix '-ness,' punctuation marks, and connectives of the sort of 'if,' 'and,' and 'or,' then there would seem to be no way in which he could consistently maintain that such terms may designate or be true of real individual entities. Imagine the suffix '-ness' or the conjunction 'if' being true of real individual entities!

32. V. "Designation and Existence," p. 47.

33. The distinction between meaning and reference is important here. *Cf.* note 31 *supra*.

34. That this particular point represents an inconsistent strain in Professor Quine's nominalism, we have already remarked in Note 31 *supra*.

35. "Designation and Existence," pp. 46-47.

36.   V. Note 31 *supra.*

37.   For an account of the genesis of Russell's
theory, *cf.* Fritz, *op. cit.,* Chapter II, Part II.
Russell himself has discussed his theory of descriptions on numerous occasions. *Cf. Introduction to Mathematical Philosophy,* Chapter
16. Also, "On Denoting" in Feigl and Sellars,
op. cit., pp. 103-118.

38.   *Cf.* Quine's statement of this: "The unana-
lyzed statement 'The author of *Waverly* was a
poet' contains a part, 'the author of Waverly,'
which is wrongly supposed by (many) to de-
mand objective reference in order to be meaningful at all.   But in Russell's translation,
'Something wrote *Waverly* and was a poet and
nothing else wrote *Waverly,*' the burden of objective reference which had been put upon a
descriptive phrase is now taken over by words
of a kind that logicians call bound variables,
variables of quantification: namely, words like
'something,' 'nothing,' everything.'   These
words, far from purporting to be names specifically of the author of *Waverly,* do not purport
to be names at all; they refer to entities generally, with a kind of studied ambiguity peculiar to themselves.   These quantificational
words or bound variables are of course a basic

part of language, and their meaningfulness, at
least in context, is not to be challenged. But
their meaningfulness in no way presupposes
there being either the author of *Waverly* or
the round square cupola of Berkeley College
or any other specifically preassigned objects."
("On What There Is," pp. 6-7).

39.   *Cf.* the quotation given in Note 38, *supra.*

40.   Again, one might protest that such a char-
acterization of Quine's nominalism does not ac-
curately represent the tenor of his views. Specifically, the objection might be directed against
my implied suggestion that Quine's ontology is
one which envisages a world of atomic individuals or ultimate simples wholly devoid of
natures and characters. And certainly, the
the evolution of semantic interpretations of
Frege's schema, as I have traced them, would
seem to lead straight from Russell's realism of
atomic individuals, plus atomic universals, to
an extreme nominalism of atomic individuals,
minus universal characteristics of any kind.

But it might be replied that Quine's nominalism just is not of a kind that involves ontological commitment to a world of character-
less atomic individuals. On the contrary, in the
Introduction to his textbook, *Methods of Logic*

(Henry Holt and Company, New York, 1950), Quine seems to repudiate anything like an ontology of atomic individuals or ultimate simples. Thus he suggests (p.XI) that "truth ordinarily attaches to statements by virtue of the nature of the world," and that "a fundamental way of deciding whether a statement is true is by comparing it, in some sense or other, with the world—or, which is the nearest we can come, by comparing it with our experience of the world."

However, Quine continues, this experience of the world which we have does not come to us in atomic bits, nor does it disclose a world made up of ultimate simples. Instead, "physical objects are known to us only as parts of a systematic conceptual structure which, *taken as a whole* (my italics), impinges at its edges upon experience." In consequence, "our statements about external reality face the tribunal of sense experience not individually but as a corporate body." (p.XII).

Admittedly, statements like these are puzzling. So far from suggesting the sort of nominalism implied by the passage quoted in Note 38, these last quoted passages are reminiscent of an almost Bradleyan type of idealism, in which Reality (or "the world" as Quine would say) becomes the ultimate subject of all judgments. Nor would I even attempt to explain how this strain in Quine's nominalism is reconcilable with the sort of nominalism which he advocates elsewhere and I have presented in the text of this lecture. In fact, I am not even sure that the former can properly be called nominalism at all. At the same time, I should hesitate to accuse Quine of inconsistency in this regard, comparable to the inconsistency mentioned in Note 31, *supra*. Rather I should think it more a case of Quine's views being still somewhat inchoate and ill-thought-out, with the result that one may hope he will devote more attention in the future to the issue of a monistic vs. a pluralistic ontology.

41.   In my book, *Intentional Logic* (Yale University Press, New Haven, 1952), I have tried to show at some length (Pt. I, pp. 20-27, and Pt. II, *passim*) that the relation of identity is peculiarly adapted for the performance of this sort of intentional function.

42.   *Cf.* St. Thomas Aquinas, *Summa contra Gentiles*, II., 75: "Nec tamen oportet quod, quia scientiae sunt de universalibus, quod universalia sint extra animam per se subsis-

tentia; sicut Plato posuit." (Editio Leonina Manualis, Rome, 1934, p. 179).

43. For an effort to treat the different predicable relationships as being all of them relations of identity, and yet as each of them intending a different sort of relation in reality, v. *Intentional Logic,* pp. 169-193.

44. In this connection I feel tempted to say that, so far as modern semantics goes, it would seem that the issue of nominalism will have to be fought out principally over these syncategorematic terms and expressions, rather than over universals of the usual sort. For supposing that contemporary nominalists can be put to rout in the matter of things like 'if's' and 'and's' and 'but's,' then one ought to have no trouble with them in the matter of universals. The reason I say this is because it would seem to be the current fashion among nominalists to try to justify their nominalism in regard to *universalia* almost exclusively in terms of their nominalism in regard to *syncategoremata.* Thus as one reads the contemporary literature, one cannot but be impressed with the extent to which modern semanticists are resorting to arguments of the following sort: since we constantly use syncategorematic words like 'if,'

'the,' 'is,' 'or' etc., quite meaningfully, and yet without ever having to suppose that there are real entities corresponding to them, why must we suppose that in order to use universal categorematic terms meaningfully, there must be real entities corresponding to them? (For instance, in Aaron's recent book this argument recurs again and again. V. *op. cit.*, pp. 127, 138, 151, 164, 166).

Now my contention is that to any argument of this sort one may make a two-pronged rejoinder. In the first place, it should be pointed out that in using syncategorematic terms like 'if' and 'or,' quite as much as in using universal categorematic terms, we do mean or intend hereby something real (although, of course, what is thus meant or intended in the use of syncategorematic terms is not the same sort of thing as is meant or intended in the use of universal categorematic terms. Thus, for example, while a categorematic term might be supposed to mean or intend an essence or nature or quiddity of something, a syncategorematic term like 'if' or 'because' or 'since' might be supposed to signify or intend some sort of causal dependence of one thing or another.)

On the other hand, and correspondingly, it should be pointed out that just as what we

intend or mean through the use of universal
concepts is not necessarily any universal thing
or entity, so also, when we use syncategorematic expressions like 'if' and 'or,' what we
mean or intend by them does not have to be a
real 'if' or 'or' *in rerum natura,* corresponding
to the logical 'if's' and 'or's' in the mind.

Moreover, having thus yielded to one
temptation, let me go further and yield to a
second and even more serious one, by saying
that just as it would seem to be that the primary issue raised by modern nominalism turns
on this question of syncategorematic terms,
so also it would seem to me that in this very
respect modern nominalism is rather different
from the sort of nominalism one is accustomed
to associate with the name of William of
Ockham. For if one accepts the interpretations
of Ockham that have been offered either by
Mr. E. A. Moody or by M. Paul Vignaux (and
I am certainly not competent to judge of the
adequacy of either of these), one of the prin-
cipal motives behind Ockham's nominalism
was apparently his conviction that the unity of
the concrete existing individual could not be
maintained, if any sort of real counterpart to
universal concepts existed in these individuals
(*Cf.* the article, *Nominalisme,* by M. Vignaux

in the *Dictionnaire de Théologie catholique,*
Paris, 1931, vol. XI, col. 733-789. V. also his
Nominalisme au XIVe siecle, Conférence Albert le Grand, Montreal and Paris, 1948, esp.
pp. 73ff.). Accordingly, Ockham was concerned to insist that although there were universal intentions in the mind, what was intended by such universals could be nothing
but particulars pure and simple. (*Cf.* E. A.
Moody, *The Logic of William of Ockham,*
Sheed and Ward, London, 1935, pp. 50-52,
56-65).

In contrast, a modern nominalist like Quine
does not seem to be particularly concerned
with Ockham's problem of the unity of the individual in the face of the reality of universals.
Nor does he consider it to be particularly in-
cumbent upon him to explain how universal intentions in the mind can none-the-less intend
individuals pure and simple. Rather he is for
the most part quite content to regard universal
concepts as not meaning or referring to anything real at all. (But *cf.* note 31 *supra.*) Instead they signify merely other concepts or
other words. In Aaron's terms (*op. cit.,* p. 136)
"what is referred to lies inward and not out-
ward; it is subjective and not objective." All
this makes me wonder whether modern nom-

inalism, as typified by Quine, may not be of a very different sort from the nominalism of a William of Ockham.

45. For an interesting and in certain respects quite contrary contemporary view, *cf.* Gilbert Ryle, *The Concept of Mind,* Hutchinson's University Library, London, 1949, pp. 120-123.

46. *Cf. Intentional Logic, op. cit.,* pp. 304-312.

47. This paragraph should be understood as merely offering a proposal rather than as laying claim to an accomplishment. For so far as I know, no one has undertaken to show in detail how the various logical relationships between propositions — conjunction, disjunction, conditionality, etc.—all of them exemplify the principle of intentionality, in a way analogous to its exemplification in the case of universal concepts. For just as *through* the relation of universality in the concept, we are enabled to intend or know a real 'what' or essence, which as such does not involve a relation of universality at all, so also it should be possible to show that *through* a logical disjunction of propositions, say, one is enabled to arrive at a knowledge of a real situation *in rerum natura* in which there is no such logical disjunction of one element from another.

But as I say, no one seems to have attempted any such demonstration of intentionality for logical relationships between propositions. To be sure, Russell in his later book, *Human Knowledge: Its Scope and Limits* (Simon and Schuster, New York, 1948) has attempted to show (pp. 119-129) that such things as negation and disjunction of propositions indicate mere subjective psychological states of the persons using such propositions, but in no wise intend any objective aspects of the situations the propositions are supposed to be about. Quite obviously, however, this latest view of Russell's only serves to point up his complete obliviousness to anything like a principle of intentionality in logic. For him it would seem that either there must be a correspondence between logical disjunction (or negation) and real disjunction, or else such disjunction must be regarded as signifying nothing real or objective at all.

48. For the text, v. Note 42 *supra.*

49. "Quamvis enim ad veritatem cognitionis necesse sit ut cognitio rei respondeat, non tamen oportet ut idem sit modus cognitionis et rei." *Op. cit.,* p. 179.

The Aquinas Lectures

Published by the Marquette University Press,
Milwaukee 3, Wisconsin

St. Thomas and the Life of Learning (1937) by
the late Fr. John F. McCormick, S.J., professor of philosophy at Loyola University.

St. Thomas and the Gentiles (1938) by Morti-
mer J. Adler, Ph.D., associate professor of
the philosophy of law, University of Chicago.

St. Thomas and the Greeks (1939) by Anton C.
Pegis, Ph.D., president of the Pontifical Institute of Mediaeval Studies, Toronto.

The Nature and Functions of Authority (1940)
by Yves Simon, Ph.D., professor of philosophy of social thought, University of Chicago.

St. Thomas and Analogy (1941) by Fr. Gerald
B. Phelan, Ph.D., director of the Mediaeval
Institute, University of Notre Dame.

St. Thomas and the Problem of Evil (1942) by
Jacques Maritain, Ph.D., professor of philosophy, Princeton University.

Humanism and Theology (1943) by Werner
Jaeger, Ph.D., Litt.D., "university" professor,
Harvard University.

The Nature and Origins of Scientism (1944) by Fr. John Wellmuth, S.J., Chairman of the Department of Philosophy, Xavier University.

Cicero in the Courtroom of St. Thomas Aquinas (1945) by the late E. K. Rand, Ph.D., Litt.D., LL.D., Pope Professor of Latin, *emeritus,* Harvard University.

St. Thomas and Epistemology (1946) by Fr. Louis-Marie Régis, O.P., Th.L., Ph.D., director of the Albert the Great Institute of Mediaeval Studies, University of Montreal.

St. Thomas and the Greek Moralists (1947, Spring) by Vernon J. Bourke, Ph.D., professor of philosophy, St. Louis University, St. Louis, Missouri.

History of Philosophy and Philosophical Education (1947, Fall) Étienne Gilson of the Académie française, director of studies and professor of the history of mediaeval philosophy, Pontifical Institute of Mediaeval Studies, Toronto.

The Natural Desire for God (1948) by Fr. William R. O'Connor, S.T.L., Ph.D., professor of dogmatic theology, St. Joseph's Seminary, Dunwoodie, N. Y.

St. Thomas and The World State (1949) by Robert M. Hutchins, Chancellor of The University of Chicago.

Methods in Metaphysics (1950) by Fr. Robert J. Henle, S.J., Dean of tthe Graduate School, St. Louis University, St. Louis, Missouri.

Wisdom and Love in St. Thomas Aquinas (1951) by Étienne Gilson of the Académie française, director of studies and professor of the history of mediaeval philosophy, Pontifical Institute of Mediaeval Studies, Toronto.

The Good in Existential Metaphysics (1952) by Elizabeth G. Salmon, associate professor of philosophy in the Graduate School of Fordham University.

St. Thomas on the Object of Geometry (1953) by Vincent Edward Smith, Ph.D., professor of philosophy, Notre Dame University.

Realism and Nominalism Revisited (1954) by Henry Veatch, Ph.D., professor of philosophy, Indiana University.

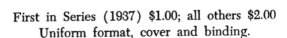

First in Series (1937) $1.00; all others $2.00 Uniform format, cover and binding.